Door In The Wall

Gerald McCarthy

Spuyten Duyvil
New York City

© 2020 Gerald McCarthy
ISBN 978-1-949966-64-0
Cover photograph: Nicholas J. Pappas

Library of Congress Cataloging-in-Publication Data

Names: McCarthy, Gerald, 1947- author.
Title: Door in the wall / Gerald McCarthy.
Description: New York City : Spuyten Duyvil, [2019] |
Identifiers: LCCN 2019051581 | ISBN 9781949966640 (paperback)
Subjects: LCGFT: Poetry.
Classification: LCC PS3563.A25917 D66 2019 | DDC 811/.54--dc23
LC record available at https://lccn.loc.gov/2019051581

for Michele
and our sons—
Nicholas. Benjamin, Nathaniel and Luke

Contents

One

Hale Eddy   3
West Corners   6
Riverhurst   7
On a line by Miguel Hernandez   9
Burdock   11
Teasel   12

Two

Flag Burning   17
The wren's nest by my kitchen window   18
Death Ship   19
Brass Buttons   21
Letter to my brother…   23
Praise song for my father   24
Home   25
Asters   26

Three

Some lines for Amy Winehouse   31
The same old song   32
Tattoo removal   33
Definitions for an election year   34
War story   35
Waking in the dark   36
Looking for the moon   38
Mountain phlox   39
Wild chicory   40

An inflated tear   42
A screen door and a cicada   43
Lines inspired by Huidobro   44
The guest   45
A bridge   46

Four

The Hooded Legion   49
The tear   50
Spring rain   51
On a line by Li Po   52
Morning glory   53
Slip away   54
Discarded armies   55
American sunset   56
Punchdrunk in Gaza   59
S.O.S   60
The clouds in the lake   61

~ ~ ~

Appendix

Fragments from Varysburg   65

But the man who comes back through the Door in the Wall will never be quite the same as the man who went out. He will be wiser but less cocksure, happier but less self-satisfied, humbler in acknowledging his ignorance yet better equipped to understand the relationship of words to things...
        Aldous Huxley

ONE

Hale Eddy (or *the recognition*)

I think you will
         know
now   in this late hour

how long it's taken us
         to find
a narrows, a coming to

where light grows
and the shade
         develops

as you might say—
what could I even
         bring you
but what you did not

         want
grief, unsmiling
even in the first light

         a glow
growing
off the morning river

         a silence
broken
by jays
         by mourning doves

gulls straying
upriver from the sea

        how far is it

to the end of

this strand

where we are now

what we have become
                      now

         holding fast
to what?

Not this rain
coming on
         a spring squall

a night wind
a dark
         lifting us

with its caress—
will you still wait

         will you

notice this change
a newness

why has it taken
so long
         to learn

the simplest of things

          the turn
towards you
without rancor

          without
anger, or
doubt, even now

          without

stars, without
some kind of guidon.

Here, the wild mustard
throws its
          yellow

in clusters and we pause
waiting again
          for the new

waiting with a kind
of awe, caught by

          the light

by some wild violets
on the edge
          spreading.

West Corners

I had almost forgotten
the afternoon in early June,
    my grandfather
fishing with us on West Creek—
my younger brother and me,
    how old were we?
Maybe my young friend
    is right, memory
is a locked drawer in a desk
and we search for the key,
    instead the drawer falls apart—
what's left are fragments,
    slivers of wood
and glass, yet we keep
trying to fit those pieces
    back together,
the sunlight coming through
overhanging trees,
    water moving over stones
water spiders skidding
    in the shadows
and his voice so far away
I can barely hear him call *listen,*
    come close—
his hands covering our hands,
    guiding us.

Riverhurst

The graves are still there.

Out beyond the black
wrought-iron fence

the Susquehanna blossoms
brown and muddy in August heat.

Down where the creek empties out
into the river, the voices of boys

shout, fishing for carp on the river's edge—
running along the shore.

Or do I just imagine them—
their voices rising in the afternoon haze?

Summer was never long enough,
or the work that came with it, never ending.

No one remembers, not Marty
who ran the pumping station, walked

the valley's rim until the houses
glowed like sparks from an engine's path.

He hung himself in his own garage,
two years after his wife took sick.

He knew anger
was no remedy for grief.

Today a young boy runs ahead of me
pauses to ask—*is this the one?*

I remember the night you pulled me
through the Labor-day crowds

to watch the stars explode—
an end to summer.

I am half in love with this memory
of you, half in love with what

I cannot get back,
what I never really had to begin with—

You know, down there in the deep current,
where the river god sleeps—

another world comes back
surfacing in eddies of foam.

A world where
hope rises like some hidden spring.

Here, he says, here it is—
I hold his hand, the two of us together

stare at the marker, red geraniums
against the white stone.

On a line by Miguel Hernandez
Mi corazón no puede con la carga

Is it the snow blurring the letters,
the snow drifting
           like a line of gray clouds
among the markers?

It does not stop.
           And I know I've come back again
as if your name in stone
could bring more than this breath
           this blur of something moving,
your shadow so late at night
coming for me.

           Once in Sintra in a stone parapet—
I heard the notes of a flute
rise in the air, and startled, thinking
           I was alone there,
I turned to see two lovers
descend the stone stair—
           one dark, the other fair.
They did not notice me,
and as the evening sea came in
           I dreamt of you, your silver fingers
turned to water, air.
We must have dreamed together
           you and I, I remember

touching your dark hair,
the snow filling up the backyards,
           the first cold flakes on my mouth.

Oh, I have gone asking for you,
embracing what I could
           as the first green deepened the still fields.

No, it's not the snow
drifting here among the stones,
           only the smoke from the caretaker's fire
as he burns last fall's leaves
along the iron fence.

for my mother, Marie 1913-1952

Burdock

Remember when summer
clung to you like cotton,

like the barbed wire fence
you pulled up,

crossing into an open meadow
the creek misted over

from the morning's rain—
and it felt as if you could run all day,

past the sheds
down through pine woods.

Memory, the doctor says—
is not a mirror,

you look away
from what you think

you saw and rediscover
something else.

Like some fingers
pulling at your sleeve,

a kind of blue—
you keep seeing just out of reach.

Teasel

If you hold anything long enough
there's bound to be trouble.
It will break apart
a little cup of light,
a sound of rain in open fields.

If you find this spiny flower
pick it up, remember
another fall, a time when the cold
came too quickly and caught
the weeds too—
the frost rising into mist,
the mist disappearing.

Today catnip and henbit,
wood sorrel, chicory
and broomsedge,
and still you keep looking
for its crown of thorns,
a blue dash in fallen leaves
above the culvert edge.

You know the railroad bed leads
to the creek, and the creek opens
out into the river, and the river
moves southward toward the sea.
At night, you listen for the trooper cars—

the sirens circling the neighborhood,
a convict in the marsh.
You think he must have got away
that prisoner,

the man they chased through
river nettles
as the season turned cold.
The morning paper
ran a photograph of the river,
night-lights and search boats.

Today, walking above stone paths
you see the pale blue streak
in the brown woods
and you know it's there.

Two

Flag burning   (a prayer)

The Sherente of South America
believe the stars
are their dead children
who have climbed into the sky.
Let each star
be a hundred children,
a thousand.
Let their innocence
keep rising above us
so we may remember
who we are, how we came here.
Let the clear cold air
be filled with them,
because the names have fallen
off the old pictures now,
and the newsreels have faded.
As another autumn
turns toward winter,
and we pause to look skyward,
hoping to glimpse Orion's belt
or Cassiopeia,
let us pray to remember
these lies we've lived with
for so long, in such earnest.

The Wren's Nest by My Kitchen Window

Today in the summer heat
a white flame burns
a secret place where grief lives.

The house wren doesn't know this—
she sings her song in the dusk
flies to her nest of twigs & bark
in the geraniums
below the window ledge.

A young man is killed,
the heat keeps us inside.
It's not enough to face it, read a book
pull up a gray hoodie
& walk out into the early dark.

It's not enough to stop
to sit still, listen to the wren
feeding her young.
Call me. Call me back.
Let me know you're all right,
let me know you're there.

No one answers, no one calls.
A night wind rises in the red oak
heat lightning in a starless sky—
we have eaten this crust of hatred,
it becomes our daily bread.

Death ship

For each flower you pick
I will bring you a body—
           a handful of blue monkshood
    for an arm,

goldenrod for eyes blinded by fire.

Here, these legs for a field of poppies,
      or a meadow of summer grass.

A simple cargo, moving shifting with the
waves.

For the sandburs scattered on a beach,
      fingers and a few toes.

Cut flowers, like hydrangea
      and I can offer up the knees,
even ankles trapped in mud.

For purple loosestrife or those clusters of
      Queen Anne's Lace

I will bring you a pile of fingernails
      some so tiny and fragile
they feel like the wings
      of flying ants.

For the sweet smell of clover
      and clumps of field grass

I will bring you the hands, fingers that ache from
weather,
hands of all sizes—

watch as they climb the cargo nets
free at last to go.
        Start now, start counting:

bring me the slender stalks of late summer wheat
        moving in the wind,

or even the breath of
        lavender,

the hum of bees trapped forever
        in the faint blue petals.

Brass Buttons

Maybe memory lies
sprawling
        upright— over
meadows,
returning in a scent of
yellow
        fragmented,
        its leaves lobed,
        lance-shaped
        piercing
        us with time.

Yet fragrant like
dogwood,
        or the damp
        of early summer rain, *memory*
is the one thing
        in the mind,
yes, but the touch too
        has
        a familiar taint
                as if joy and
        pain were in
the surface of things—

a kiss in late afternoon,
        a lake in the distance
and the day itself
        only a glimpse
blurred by our own
                failing

as if a selectiveness
    were hidden in the skin,
    the sweetness of jasmine

on the tongue, to start, *to*
    make a start for in the

        beginning
            there is a freshness—
        a wakening even,

            the open marshland
            rising with yellow light.

Letter to my brother
from the Onondaga County Jail

In the snow, in the blinding snow—
I thought of you
the sullen, gray winter day
they brought me there.

Handcuffed, shackled
I wondered what you would think
if you could have seen me:

stumbling into the long cellblock—
in my winter dress green uniform
trying to seem aloof, hard-edged,
I had just turned twenty.

Now I wonder where you were
that winter—
did you know where they'd taken me?
Did you know I never even said
Goodbye—

I say it now—*Goodbye*,
there's grace in that,
the way time has of fooling us
of fouling up the mechanics

of our lives—so we learn too late
how precious the hours are,
how I wish you might
have seen me then,
how alone and lost I felt without you.

Praise song for my father

What I miss now is not the dark
it's the light, the cone of light
coming from a table lamp,
my father sitting at the plain deal table
paying the bills in a shuffle of papers.
I see him drinking a cup of coffee
staring out
at the back yard—
it's a September night
and I have to get up for school,
but I watch him—
running his hands through his hair
sipping the coffee,
as if he hears a kind of song
out there in the night's dark,
a music only he remembers.
The night's coolness,
the sound of crickets
and the freights slowing for
the North Side loading dock—
helps him forget the bills, the work.
For a few moments he sings the song to
himself and he's far away.
Praise the early fall dark,
praise the cool night that lets my father dream,
singing his own song again.
Praise my father for
the things he gave up and lost,
and could not get back.

Home

A factory town,
the color of the sky
is smoke.
Smoke is the way
day began—
an anger bred
of work and tiredness
crept in with the smoke.
In winter, homes
were lit early—
the snow drifted
beneath streetlights
and hundred-year-old maples.
The bread man came
door to door,
and kitchens smelled
of semolina bread all night.
Downtown the smoke
stays, curls in factory bars,
lingers in the gray drifts
of steep streets.
Winter is gray, dark gray,
below the steel bridge—
the river churns with ice.
Smoke lives in the air,
the taste of soot
is on your tongue
and when you speak—
it is the language of smoke.

Asters

Even now in this winter dusk
even in this cold,
you see them,
        white clusters
like drops of mist.

No one knows why
they are still here
        in roadside gullies, near
spruce and fallen ash,
growing along
        the edge of concrete posts,
        railroad ties.

Star clusters
like the breath of sleep,
        or what—hope?

No, nothing lasts
        nothing stays the same.
Even now these tiny stars
        tease us with the memory
of days, sunset days.

You can't go back.
        This road song stays
a glimpse of white
against the brown fields,
        along the stone wall's edge.

Is it in this we are taken?
        A glance unsure yet certain
they are still here.

Steelweed
        the farmer calls them,
white heath asters

rising along the rim of
days, along the edge of
        winter. Even now, even in
this cold.

Three

Some lines for Amy Winehouse (in the rain)

The first time I heard Mary Wells sing
The one who really loves you—

I was eighteen in a place called Tam Ky
where it rained for two months straight.

I learned how to dance there
in the rain, listening to *soul* music

trying to get my shoulders into it.
Soul brothers taught me—singing back up

doing the dap, the drop down, dancing
together. Now your voice brings back that fall

the songs I learned—too young to know
their lyrics would last, like loss does and longing.

There's that, and the rain today in the wild roses
a summer rain this time, and *I wake up alone*—

THE SAME OLD SONG

The night the crackers burned a cross
in front of Doc Brown's tent,

Turner and I pulled the late guard, watched
as the smoke rose over the company yard,

and I could sense his anger across the close dark
of our sandbagged hole,

when he sighed—I knew
they'd get around to this.

Staring through the starlight scope,
I thought I saw that burning cross

spread its flames beyond
the headlands, reddening the sky—

until dawn took me by surprise, raw daylight
settling around us like a wound.

Tattoo removal

First, take the one from the fall
I turned eighteen—
Death before
Dishonor
      a blue sword and a snake.
Take the deaths it would know
      so many boys falling
      like the leaves of maples on
the street where I grew up.
Next, take the heart and flowers from
the summer of *love*—
      remove the slow dance
      of candles, the other deaths,
different and public,
    forcing us to look up,
startled by the light.
Take these swirls of
      blue and black and red—
remove these emblems from
      a time of insolence and greed.
Give me instead this clear dark,
      untouched and liquid.
Give me the pale shoulders,
      the fierce embrace of days—
the full breath of fall wisteria
still blooming in the chill.

DEFINITIONS FOR AN ELECTION YEAR

Grief was the name of my friends' dog—
a black Labrador that ran off
along the shores of Lake Michigan,
the summer I turned twenty-eight.

Hope is green, my grandfather said,
like the spring, and Hope
the name of a woman
you knew in Iowa, someone
who promised dinner
and a cool drink. You got the drink.

Sleep is a dark hood
you pull over your head
when the night comes
and there are only stars.

Truth, the general said,
is varied—truth has a slow fuse.
No, truth is the one thing
*it touches all things
that touch the heart.*

War Story

At the garbage dump
the air fills with flies,
you hear the droning sigh
above the truck's motor,
the cries of children
fighting for scraps of food,
tin cans, shreds of clothing.
Jenkins laughs, pushes
the fifty-gallon drum over
the tailgate.
The children shout,
surge toward us.
Watch this, he says,
tipping the other drum on its side,
it splashes down, covers them
in coffee grounds, stale bread,
egg shells.

Waking in the Dark

They kept their watch
in the blue dark —

the nursing station light
with its single yellow eye.

Call us brothers of the blue robe,
brothers of the broken blade.

We were the lucky ones
who got away, who made our peace

— *necessary as air.*
There, through steel screens

we saw the harbor—the open sea
teasing us with distance.

On the locked ward, our racks
chained like coffins on a ship's deck,

tilting, twenty to a row—
awash in *what might have been.*

Sleep came with a lozenge
dissolved in a suffocating swiftness.

They gave us what we learned to crave—
dreams in fistfuls of yellow caps.

Dawn came early—call it dread
biting each of us with its tongue of light.

Call it morning—rose red
but blue seems more like it— the head nurse

calling for the corpsmen—a sergeant
locked in a shower stall with a stolen razor.

Like a dark thread those beds
still spin their labyrinth of night—

What chrysalis for those
who came through?

Looking for the Moon

From my son I have learned
to look at the sky again,
to cherish such simple things—

this leaf fallen to the curb
spreading its web of color in his hand,
the pinecone nestled in the grass,
opening, and this one life

culled from so many years of anger,
surfacing now in late fall.

As he gives me his hand
he asks—where's the moon?

Oh, how can I tell him
of that other world,
the stupid cruelty of men
who should have known better?

It's there—rising above the houses,
the river, throwing its pale glow
over us, as if together
the two of us might rise above this life.

Mountain phlox

There's a blue that rises
above the blueness
as if the world could return
      in blue—
Hey, he said—*let's go,*
      let's not look back.

You remember
an afternoon
by a roadside,
waiting for the day to give way
to evening—all the while
listening to the papery sound
of grasshoppers
      the fresh cut hay wafting
over the scent of shadowy blue.

From one war to another—
      you've grown old,
learning so little from mistakes,
except to say you've made them.

This one hand opening
against the cool night,
this door, this light on the transom,
this remembrance of blue—

for Robert Bohm

Wild Chicory

Blue sailors you called them—slim petals
like the spokes of a wheel

opening for a few hours in
the waste places.

Yet now when I think of you,
it's the snow I see—

a winter's night
we crossed the frozen lake in a storm.

Yes, I know the lights led us on
the ice moaned, thickening

like the almost human cry
of someone lost.

Today my sons and I walk the berm
of the river road,

they kneel in deep grass and I call out, afraid
of things unseen—broken bottles, tin cans.

But turning his face to me my youngest son
says—*flowers for mom.*

Wild chicory pulled from
the roadside.

Blue sailors I tell him,
named for someone who did not return.

And walking back along the way we've come,
it starts to snow

a river squall blown southward
my sons laughing in the sudden flurry.

And for a moment I see your face again—
the taste of wet snow on your mouth,

a time when it seemed
we had the whole way clear.

An inflated tear

after Rahsaan Roland Kirk

When we left you
in the wet dank of the March morning,
I had to read some words over you.

Read this the priest said
instead I read those lines from Hernandez—
you are gone now.

Now far from the place where you were born,
I watch the mist rise over the ridge,
your brothers asleep in the hammock's sway.

The leaves drag across the tiles
and I remember that morning of rain,
wondering how I can ever listen to the rain

without speaking your name,
here in these fitful mists that cling to the oaks
like smoky webs, even here, each day,

each morning brings back
a glimpse of you—my heart's song,
my long, lost life.

A screen door and a cicada

Whenever I see maple leaves pressed
like tiny welts of color in wet streets—
I think of my father's anger.

A screen door slams, a boy leaps
off the stoop of a back porch,
runs into the early dark on West Main.

Later he scuttles away from the belt,
pushes into the corner of his room,
a bright glare when the bed is pulled back.

At school the next day
he feels the fiery ribbons
pushing his back against the wooden chair slats.

Today, angry snarls of leaf blowers
shatter the still heat. A landscaper
clears the grass cuttings in the neighbor's yard.

My son carries the carapace of a cicada
cradled in his hand —*look at this Dad*, he says,
the brown body curled in on itself.

(for Billy Collins)

Lines inspired by Huidobro

Let the world go
you can't save it.
Let the waves crash
over the breakwater
        let the storm break—
you can't stop it.

Let the young girl go—
she's gone anyway
        her family carries her
with its own grief.

Let the boy go too—
it's been almost a year
        his song stays with you.

You can't do anything
about the ones you've lost.

You can't forget them,
you can't stop carrying them—
        like a weight, a backpack
full of names, each one
polished by time.

The Guest

Grief comes in the door
uninvited
like some gust of wind
or a neighbor who pushes his way in
and refuses to go—
everything is moved
to make room for him.

It's in the leaves dragging across the roof,
scraping against the stone path
like the shuffle of someone
we can no longer see—

Loss piles up like a sleeplessness,
the night sound of branches
rubbing along the gutters.

The snow sifts down over the fields—
a dust of stars, silent, still.

We look away,
across the open places
believing we can forget
the hard edge of hours.
It's no use—it's there
like some old cracked cup
one we must drink from
again and again.

A BRIDGE

Say it's November
and you want your life back—
you want to walk out
past those bare trees
see how late it is,
how much time has passed.

Call it a fall dream—
call it the way you happen to be,
the way you feel looking up
at the stars—

Say it's just now starting to snow
and the cold air
welcomes you back, the moon
rising over all of it—
a sail moving through bare branches.

As if you too were adrift,
unanchored
like some junk floating
into the waves of a storm.

Say death comes up like that—
unexpected, someone prodding you
like hey, what's this?
A tiny irritation,
a small lump beneath the skin.
It goes from bad to worse,
and you keep on asking.

Four

The Hooded Legion

> *let us put up a monument to the lie*
> Joseph Brodsky

There are no words here
to witness why we fought,
who sent us or what we hoped to gain.

There is only the rain
as it streaks the black stone,
these memories of rain
that come back to us—
a hooded legion reflected in a wall.

Tonight we wander weaponless and cold
along the shore of the Potomac
like other soldiers who camped here
looking out over smoldering fires into the night.

What did we dream of
the summer before we first went away?
What leaf did not go silver
in the last light?
What hand did not turn us aside?

The tear

It starts with just a small rip
a slight torn place on the collar,
grows until
the collar itself is gone,
the threads hang down
like tiny rivulets.

It's not enough to say
you'll wear a torn place
on your sleeve,
you'll call and wait
for them to hear you
calling—

It's not enough to know
you can't stop this dying
this living,
no, not enough to know
he was right, the poet of broom
and stark hills—
love and death are of
the same mother,
and now all these ghosts
return, sewn onto a shoulder
like stars,
or a chevron,
a badge you cannot remove.

Spring rain

Today in the morning news
headlines tell of more war—

the mourning dove calls
out back near the compost pile—

rain in the wild violets,
their deep blue reminds me of you—

this year there are thick clusters
beneath the shade of the spruce

so many blue flowers glisten—
I can't believe you are gone.

On a line by Li Po

Second snow of November,
already
the high peaks white
in the blue distance.

Another November comes back—
my first homecoming,
bent double,

carrying twin duffels down
from a train,
city lights, the war far away.

Tonight, my sons stand beside me
poking the fire, wet snow
melting in embers.

The great horned owl's cry
pierces the dark,
and I think *of what ruins our lives.*

Morning glory

Now, it becomes
the things in between—
all the mornings
I have watched you wake
like a pale shadow
of grace
as if a shadow waited
outside
in the glow—
Wait, you can see
rainwater reflected
on a roof,
you can smell the rain
even now—
It's you
in the deep blue
of morning,
it's just you,
reminding me
what I love is close by,
twisting upward
toward the light.

Slip Away

Sorry, it becomes a kind of chant
if you say it over
and over again.

I'm sorry, sorry—
and only sorrow comes
waiting at the weathered gray door,

a barn door, opening
into the brown fields of fall
your grandfather calls—

everything's a dream
and then he's gone, rising
like some giant winged bird

above the still fields
and sorry is not just a word any longer—
it becomes a part of you

like a gnarled iron root
and only the song—growing
slip away, slip away.

Discarded Armies

Fires burn, smolder in old oil drums
the smoke folds over us—
Hey man—got a smoke?
Got a dollar? Something to keep
the cold out? Something
to take away?

Their names rise
like mist—and no one
counts cadence.
Call it what you will,
call it 10-58
out of service, broke down
busted. Call it *S.O.S.*
that's what Sonia wrote—
please reply soon.
A song someone starts to sing
carry me—come to
carry me.

Fires burn, wood smoke
thick and deep like syrup—
like wine,
like a letter you keep trying to write—

American Sunset, Attica

for Gil Scott-Heron

The rain has no memory of September,
but I remember the rain,
the dark nights of rain,
gray morning light, turkey vultures
circling above the locust trees—
rain, pooling in the yards.

And the rain falling
blood mixed with dirt and gravel.

Your voice asking—
kick it, quit it—but did you ever try?

Today in the spring snow
the roads come back—white roads
roads of snow and ice
and I hear your voice
asking—*did you ever try?*

Keeplock, lock-up, the box,
the hole,
slow-down, strip-search
metal detector, the keys,
the locks, the gates—
doing time, keeping time, marking time.

Down, a man is down—
off the count.

Mac standing in the D block Hall—
the block where the riot began.
Mac and Akbar Ali smiling—
                reciting their poem together—one chorus
then the next:

Whose man are you? My man?
                    Your man? Whose man
are you gonna be?

Dusk falling
covering the gray walls
the towers, farm country—

small towns like Darien
Belknap, Dutch Corners.

The rain cannot remember
the roads, the names,
someone asking—*Freedom from what*?

The street, the hack
hitting the bars
with his stick.

Freedom from probation
and a thirty-dollar room,
from a PO with a hundred men
still linked by chain—
nobody's going home,
no one's got a shake.
Home is where the hatred is—
                white powder dreams.

You can't get back there now,
you can't drive a backroad
without thinking of the men,
their names ring like iron on stone
like rain puddling in the yards—
thems years, he says
and you look up, only
no one's there.

Punchdrunk in Gaza

A face we put on
in streets of rain
a face *to greet the others
that we meet*—
a cover for the locomotive of the heart,
a thin disguise
for the breathlessness
of feeling—
a way to keep sleepwalking
*turn away, turn
away,*
the world
is a cylinder of glass
and our time here
a narrow fracture
like a bridge
suspended
half way across a chasm.

S.O.S

He says—*Young people don't need
to know about Malcolm.*

*They've had enough of Black
oppression.
Those things are old hat,
 passé—*

I listen to his voice rising,
the syllables
tripping over one another,
thick cadences of sound.

Outside, the snow melts,
the roof eaves catch the sun's rays.

I think about books,
about recovery,
remember
another winter,
a time when I stood on line
to get my share
of creamed,
chipped beef on toast.
S.O.S. they called it then.

Later, standing guard on a deserted airstrip,
we got the word,
they'd gunned down Malcolm
at the Audubon Ballroom
in New York.

The corporal who poured me
my first taste of straight bourbon,
chided me
as I held out the canteen cup—
he snorted—
too young to know him,
a tense laughter easing
through our group.

A dreamer, the others said,
too young to go that way.

The night wind gusted,
furling the canvas tent flaps,
making the bare electric bulbs
flicker.

We were all too young,
and we fell to earth in places
we did not know.

But Malcolm knew—*the price
of freedom is death,*
and he did not turn aside.

Now it seems as if that February night
of stars and dark wind
rippling
the sea marsh
was a spark that lit the flames
of all the nights to follow,

the deaths linking up—pale cut-outs
burning,
until our eyes were blind with fire.

The Clouds in the Lake

A loon
out over the flow
near Chimney Rock Wilderness
in August,
summer smells
of pine woods, wild mustard,
Queen Anne's lace.

Look, Nathaniel
says—the sky's
in the water.

Appendix

Fragments from Varysburg

The islands then
the rocks at last—the moorings.

   A ship deserted in the surf
    a freighter run aground—
her decks awash
with ocean scum and algae.

   A morning when we climbed aboard
found traces of the haste
her crew had left in,
   heard water slosh in
    empty compartments,
left to break up in the waves.

 The headlands then
rain steaming inland up the coast
   the signals of passage—
the harbor and coming back
the leavings,
   a thirst for leaving.

*

This ship left
rolling in the surf,
and when the swells came—
pushed hard up
against the rocks
by wind in sudden storm.

A ship that seemed—
a respite—
from sudden shock of sound
metal runway strips, planes landing
in dark roars
heat rising with the first light—
the smell of age, of decay
of salt-spray
the rolling feel of the rusted decks
the swing and pitch
of time.

The Sherente of South America
have a myth to explain
the origin of the stars.

It remains the story of the hunter,
we can see his severed leg
in the sky—
Orion's belt.

Image creates its own
illusion—   real singing
a wind in god.

*

Well gentlemen they sd:
      we take the first three dreams
you have
and call them memory.
                You never dream anything else.

They listened
the sound of voices,
in nightstorm of ocean
notes rising in the air.

Outward—
beneath the glow of ash sky,
they counted the bridges
to the sea.

*

Would recall Glaucus
who wrote:
men in their generations
are as the leaves—

A fear caught up with them
a worm that burrowed deep
and remained.

As the child after grief
hesitates, alone
with no one coming.

The land gives up
sends itself out in code.

*

A kind of plant whose flowers
           do not change color
or appearance   in drying—
they may be kept for years
without losing their beauty.
The French call them
Immortelles.

Listen, if you put your ear
to the earth
           you will hear the drums
the steel doors opening,
closing.   Listen,
the sound of weeping,
a pounding,
the rhythm
of a single drumbeat
stirring the waters,
stirring the dark waves—

no star woman,
no one to bring us the secrets
of maize.

*

Now having lost their way,
they asked
the same questions, again
and again

as if in the asking alone
in the repetition
      there was a kind of song—
      a song, carried forward
like a weight.
A flock of dark birds
against the winter sky
moving—
driven by wind,
against forgetting
against the islands—

  the dream of some safe haven,
              the breathing—
                    writhing thing
          hope becomes.

A sailor of circumstance
        searching
for some remnant of his crew
for some sign of his nation
reaffirmed.

I grow inward, he wrote
in the first spring.
It seemed as if he lived
on a spar of land that jutted out
into an endless sea.

Or perhaps this was only
in a dream—as if
he waited for some sign
a warning of what to do next,
where to go.

*

He felt he was lost
in the streets of a city
walking uphill, the streetlights
leading away from water.

Yellow leaves falling
in the yellow dusk—
until it seemed he was walking deeper
into a narrowing tunnel.

*In rooms bleached white
the shadow men draw in
their breath.*

"Those who go searching for love
are loveless."

*

Late the hour,
                    to come upon this again—
to note:
here, here at last I have found
what—
the dissonance of time, of these
broken syllables?

I know the way leads past it all—
marked with rectangles of gray light.

Oh, heart
here is a leaf that has not fell to earth
        the boy knows what the men cannot
        heartfelt his offering—

*

History is a dream, Arguelles wrote—
        the dream of reason.

    I have been a product of
my time (s)
fallen, broke—
              of two times two times two
  and maybe we all unknown
             are products of one
family.
He was right—
            you know,

man/woman
more interesting than nature
than this concept of god—

*

A page torn from an old notebook
        dated next to the mileage.

The ways back—
all the roads leading again
to April
like the rose pressed between pages
of a book,
or the moth caught in a spider's web
the petals   the wings
        fall apart
shadows crossing the distance
like a hand remembering the feel
of surfaces, of things
sought after
dreamed about—

*

This was the threnody then
carried like a flag,
homeward—

as if home were there
amidst
these rocks and foaming surf
as if they might wade ashore
in the rush of breakers—

but a flag to what?
to whom?

Not the past, not the memory
of that time.

Perhaps just to memory alone
then, to memory continuing
to these things they brought with them
that they have become.

*

"promise them,
say to them
anything, anything at all..." (overheard)

Snow clings to the lilac branches—
I'm nothing, he wrote
I will always be nothing.

Tonight the wind
the deep sigh
of some lake barge
bound northward
toward the St. Lawrence
and the sea.

A tear the sun lets fall—
against the stone breakwall
against the ice.

*

Outward and outward
   the motion alone, his will
       adrift in the world.

These are the sons
who have lost God—

for everything that lives is holy,
life delights in life.

*

And now the *wind-blown chaff of days*
so much to know, to
follow, to stumble upon
wondering how
it has come to this—
now, so much of
the now
they could not rise above
it, could not deny what there is with
                them.

*

He had his trade in
his hands

    they say—
    he had the shape of
things, the feel of surfaces.

As if a history were here
a history kept us here—
        the work, the long hours
and each one with
that history written in
his hands, in
her hands.

The indifference of
Spring coming again into
the trees
into this open space—
        a waking, a resolution to
keep on
waking.

Notes

The Tear is for Jesse Moses Yanko (2/16/1996-11/28/2012)

Inflated Tear is for Luke William McCarthy (2/17/1992-2/29/1992)

In "American Sunset, Attica" most of the lines in italics are from Gil Scott-Heron's song *Home Is Where The Hatred Is*.

In "Fragments from Varysburg"

Random lines in italics or quotes are from:

Rainer Maria Rilke; D. H. Lawrence; Charles Olson; Song of Amergin; Fernando Pessoa (The Scaffolding); William Blake; and The Bible/New Testament.

Acknowledgments: Thanks to the editors of the magazines and anthologies where some of these poems originally appeared or were reprinted:

The North American Review— "War Story" (as War Story #13)
America— "Praise Song for My Father"
The Beloit Poetry Journal— "Flag Burning"
TriQuarterly— "The Hooded Legion"
North Dakota Quarterly— "Teasel" (new version)
Hawaii Pacific Review and *Hawaii Pacific Review—Best of the Decade* "The Same Old Song"
Third Wednesday— "Tattoo Removal," "Wild Chicory" and "Lines inspired by Huidobro"
Mobile City— "Patriotism"
Radius: Poetry from the Center to the Edge "The death ship"
i70 Review— "Asters" "Salvage" and "Brass Buttons"
Flying Horse— "Looking for the moon"
The Chaffin Review— "Punchdrunk in Gaza"
Blue Collar Review "Home"
The Pedestal Magazine "Mountain Phlox"
Two of Cups Press "A Bridge"
The Café Review— "Definitions for an election year," "Some lines for Amy Winehouse" and "Slip Away"
Italian Americana—"The clouds in the lake"
An Outbreak of Peace/Arachne Press—(England) "Burdock"
The Deadly Writers Patrol –"Discarded Armies" and "Letter to my brother from the Onondaga County Jail"
Signor No –an international anthology against war " On a line by Li Po"(as "A proposito di una riga di Li Po") Roma, 2010; edited by Marco Cinque e Phil Rushton

In addition "The Hooded Legion" was reprinted in *TriQuarterly-20th Anniversary Anthology* and *The New Anthology of Contemporary Poetry: Postmodernisms 1950-present* (Rutgers University Press)

A few sections of "Fragments from Varysburg" were originally published in *House Organ* edited by Kenneth Warren

Waging Peace in Vietnam-US soldiers and veterans who opposed the war (NYU Press, 2019) "Letter to my brother from the Onondaga County Jail"

My sincere thanks to David and Sylvia Kelly—who helped me come all the way home. And John Crawford and Richard Martin for their support and encouragement.

I am also grateful to The American Academy in Rome for a Visiting Artist residency in Spring 2016 that allowed me to complete some of the poems in this collection.

GERALD MCCARTHY's books include *War Story (1977), Shoetown (1992)* and *Trouble Light (2008).* A Marine veteran who served with the 1st Combat Engineer Battalion in Vietnam, he worked in the Endicott-Johnson shoe factories before attending SUNY Geneseo and the Iowa Writers Workshop. He has taught writing in schools, colleges, migrant labor camps, jails, and Attica Prison.

A recipient of grants and awards from the NEH, the NYS Council on the Arts, the National Writers Union, the Gilder Lehrman Center for American History and the NAACP-Spring Valley Chapter; McCarthy also has had three Visiting Artist residencies at the American Academy in Rome. His poetry and writing have appeared in numerous anthologies and magazines including: *From Both Sides Now* (Scribners), *Warrior Writers/ New Jersey, Postmodernisms* (Rutgers Univ. Press), *American War Poetry* (Oxford University Press), *Carrying the Darkness, A New Geography of Poets, We Gotta Get Out of This Place* (Univ. of Massachusetts Press), *TriQuarterly, America, Nimrod, New Letters, Ploughshares,* and *The Café Review.*

He is currently at work on a memoir— *Vet, Deconstructed.*

https://en.wikipedia.org/wiki/Gerald_McCarthy_(poet)

https://geraldmccarthypoet.website/

www.ingramcontent.com/pod-product-compliance
Lightning Source LLC
Chambersburg PA
CBHW060538080526
44586CB00012B/783